S0-ADL-798

THREE DIMENSIONAL SHAPES

SPHERES

Luana K. Mitten

Rourke
Publishing LLC
Vero Beach, Florida 32964

www.rourkepublishing.com

PHOTO CREDITS: © ZoneCreative: page 7 top; © Russell McBride: page 15 top; © Jon Helgason: page 15 bottom, 17; © George Bailey: page 19 top, 21; © Yamac Beyter: page 19 bottom; © Richard Hobson: page 22 rght; © Feng Yu: page 23 top; © ranplett: page 23 bottom;

Editor: Kelli Hicks

Cover design by Nicola Stratford, bdpublishing.com

Interior Design by Heather Botto

Library of Congress Cataloging-in-Publication Data

Mitten, Luana K.
  Three dimensional shapes : spheres / Luana K. Mitten.
    p. cm. -- (Concepts)
  ISBN 978-1-60472-413-4
  1. Sphere--Juvenile literature. 2. Shapes--Juvenile literature. 3. Geometry,
Solid--Juvenile literature. I. Title. II. Title: Spheres.
  QA491.M57 2009
  516'.156--dc22
                            2008018801

Printed in the USA

CG/CG

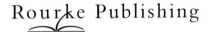

Rourke Publishing

www.rourkepublishing.com – rourke@rourkepublishing.com
Post Office Box 3328, Vero Beach, FL 32964

What makes this a sphere?

Look and you will see
a sphere is round.
No points here!

4

5

Which fruit

is a sphere?

No points here,
an orange is a sphere.

9

Which vegetable
is a sphere?

No points here,
these peas are spheres.

13

Which gum is a sphere?

14

No points here,
these gumballs
are spheres.

17

Which treat
is a sphere?

No points here,
these doughnut holes
are spheres.

21

No points here, can you find more spheres?

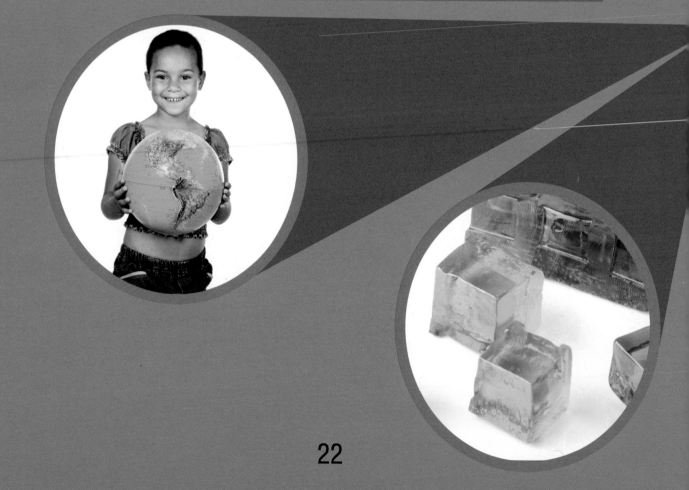

23

Index

Further Reading

Kalman, Bobbie. *What Shape is It?* Crabtree Publishing, 2007.
Senisi, Ellen B. *A 3-D Birthday Party.* Children's Press, 2006.

Recommended Websites

www.42explore.com/geomet.htm
www.atozkidsstuff.com/shpes.html
www.abc.net.au/countusin/default.htm

About the Author

Luana Mitten's house is on a golf course. She has egg cartons full of little, white spheres (golf balls) that land in her yard when the golfer's shots miss the green.